D0886558

LIVES OF IRISH ARTISTS

Walter Osborne
1859–1903

JEANNE SHEEHY

Walter Osborne
1859–1903

JEANNE SHEEHY

THE NATIONAL GALLERY OF IRELAND

Produced in 1991 by

Town House

41 Marlborough Road

Donnybrook

Dublin 4

for The National Gallery of Ireland

British Library Cataloguing in Publication Data

Sheehy, Jeanne

Walter Osborne.—(Lives of Irish artists)

1. Ireland. Paintings

I. Title II. Series

759.2

ISBN: 0-948524-23-5

Cover: *Life in the Streets, Musicians (1893)*

Title page photo courtesy of The National Gallery of Ireland

Managing editor: Treasa Coady

Series editor: Brian P Kennedy (NGI)

Text editor: Elaine Campion

Design concept: Q Design

Typeset by Printset & Design Ltd, Dublin

Printed in Italy

CONTENTS

Walter Osborne (signature)

Jeanne Sheehy was born in Dublin in 1939, the daughter of the art critic Edward Sheehy. She read modern languages at University College Dublin and took an M.Litt. at Trinity College Dublin. She studied History of Art at the École du Louvre, Paris. She is now Principal Lecturer in History of Art at Oxford Polytechnic. She is the author of *Walter Osborne* (1974), *J J McCarthy and the Gothic Revival in Ireland* (1977), *Irish Art and Architecture*, with Peter Harbison and Homan Potterton (1978), and *The Rediscovery of Ireland's Past* (1980). She compiled the catalogue for the 'Walter Osborne' exhibition at the National Gallery of Ireland and the Ulster Museum (1983).

Walter Osborne was born into a middle-class Dublin family, who lived, from his early childhood, at No. 5 Castlewood Avenue, Rathmines. His was one of those solid Protestant families that produced doctors, lawyers, clergymen, and the occasional writer or painter. William Osborne, Walter's father, was himself a painter. He had had a difficult start in life—an orphan, he was brought up by an uncle and sent to a Moravian school in Leeds, where he was very unhappy. His uncle would not countenance him becoming a painter, and he sent him to work in the offices of the merchants Ferrier Pollock in Dublin. He stuck this for a time, but meanwhile he studied art, becoming an Associate of the Royal Hibernian Academy in 1854 and a full Academician in 1868. He specialised in animal painting, mostly dogs and horses, and managed to make a modest living. The family was nationalist in its politics, and in religion tended towards high-church Anglicanism, which was most unusual in Ireland.

Early Education and
Training

Walter Osborne was educated at Rathmines School. He did not have a particularly distinguished academic career, and he seems to have left at the age of sixteen. When he decided to become a painter he was not, as his father had been, discouraged by his family. In 1876 he enrolled in the schools of the Royal Hibernian Academy. From the beginning he did brilliantly, and carried off many prizes, finishing with the Taylor Scholarship in 1881.

The schools' committee recommended that he continue his studies at an English or foreign school of art. At that time it was the custom for artists to complete their education by travelling and studying abroad—in fact it was essential to their future success. There were flourishing schools of art all over Europe, though by the late nineteenth century Paris was the most popular place for artists. Walter Osborne, however, like many of his Irish and British contemporaries, chose to go to Antwerp. It was much cheaper than Paris and, having only one school, was less confusing—Paris had a number of studios and a reputation for wickedness. The Academy at Antwerp was renowned for providing solid teaching, and many well-known painters of the day, including Ford Madox Brown and Lawrence Alma Tadema, had been trained there.

On 29 September 1881, Walter Osborne, together with his friends Nathaniel Hill and Joseph Malachy Kavanagh, registered at the Royal Academy of Fine Arts in Antwerp. Osborne was obviously fairly proficient, and was allowed to go straight into the life class, where students painted and drew from the living model; Hill and Kavanagh were obliged to spend a few weeks drawing from plaster casts of antique statues before joining the senior class.

Antwerp was indeed inexpensive. You could get lodgings, with breakfast of coffee and bread-and-butter, and dinner by arrangement with a neighbouring inn, all for about five francs a month; and tuition at the Academy was free.

The Academy itself was a lively place, and very popular with students from all over Europe and from America. Discipline was strict; classes ran from eight in the morning until twelve, with an afternoon session from one-thirty until four-thirty. If you were late, you were excluded from class. The Antwerp training put great emphasis on speed and verve of execution, and on colour. There was much attention given to the lessons to be learned from the then greatest Flemish master, Rubens. The time spent on a composition was limited usually to two hours—very different from the English or Irish system, where you slaved over a piece of work until you achieved a high degree of finish. Osborne learned to use colour imaginatively, and to turn away from the soupy brown shadows still in vogue at home. He learned to apply paint freely and energetically, but with precision. He learned the importance of carefully *11* worked-out composition, and preparatory drawing.

❧

OTHER INFLUENCES

The training at the Academy was concentrated on figure painting and heroic subject matter. But Osborne and his friends were influenced by a very different kind of Belgian painting, namely, the realism of painters who had trained in the Landscape and Animal Painting Classes at Antwerp, who painted peasant genre, and domestic interiors reminiscent of Dutch painting of the seventeenth century. Like them, the Academy students in the 1880s painted quaint corners of the city, and roamed the surrounding villages in their spare time. It was on just such an expedition that Osborne painted *Moderke Verhoft*, 'little mother'

12

Verhoft, at Calmphout, in the area known as the Campine, a favourite haunt of the Belgian realists (*Pl 1*).

Walter Osborne spent about eighteen months at the Antwerp Academy, and it was there that he laid the real foundations of his career as a painter. The teaching he got was important, as was the introduction to the work of other painters, both contemporaries and old masters. It was at Antwerp that he began to make contact with a wide circle of fellow artists. Among these was Blandford Fletcher, who had come to Antwerp from the school of art at South Kensington, London, and other English painters who were to introduce him into *plein-air* circles in England. *Plein-air* painting—where the artists worked in the open air in front of the motif, trying to capture the truth and convey the feeling of nature as they saw it—was attracting young artists all over Europe, and Osborne was no exception.

At Antwerp Osborne formed the habit of going on painting expeditions with small groups of fellow artists; in the spring of 1883, having completed his studies, he set out for Brittany, probably in the company of Blandford Fletcher and Nathaniel Hill. Brittany was then very popular with painters of all persuasions, but especially with the realists, who liked to paint the humbler aspects of rural and seafaring life and who were attracted by the picturesque costumes of Breton peasants, the sense of remote

cont. p25

ILLUSTRATIONS

PLATE 1

Moderke Verhoft *c* 1882

13

Pl 1

14

This sketch was clearly done from life. It is freely handled, yet there is a sense of underlying drawing defining the form. The paint is applied in precisely calculated strokes so that the sharp orange and gold notes of the scarf and bowl are set off by the subtler greys and blues of the skirt and shawl. The subject matter, an old Flemish peasant-woman, is typical of Belgian realism of this period.

Oil on panel; 21.1 x 13.3 cm
National Gallery of Ireland

Pl 2

Painted in Brittany, it is executed in a subtle range of greys, greens and beiges that we find in a lot of Osborne's work of the eighties. The landscape is confidently handled, but there is some awkwardness in the foreground figure, as if the painter was still finding his way. In her Breton peasant clothes, absorbed in her work, she is typical of the girls and boys Osborne chose as models at this time.

Oil on canvas; 58 x 46 cm
National Gallery of Ireland

PLATE 2

Apple Gathering, Quimperlé 1883

15

PLATE 3

An October Morning 1885

16

Pl 3   **T**he even, pale light of this picture is like other plei
air works of the period. What makes it unusual, an
suggests that the artist had been looking at the work
the French impressionists, is the painting of the pebb
on the beach in vivid touches of pure, almost pointilli
colour. This was the first picture Osborne showed at t
New English Art Club in London, where most of t
naturalist and impressionist painters exhibited.

Oil on canvas; 71.1 x 91.4 cm
Guildhall Art Gallery, Corporation of London

PLATE 4

_____

A Cottage Garden 1888

Pl 4   Painted at *Uffington, near Oxford, where Osborne
worked with Blandford Fletcher. Such a vivid and
detailed evocation of flowers is unusual for him, and
closer to Fletcher's sweeter, more sentimental style. It is
signed with the square capital letters by which, all over
Europe, the followers of Bastien-Lepage signalled their
allegiance to 'realism'.*

17

Oil on canvas; 67 x 49 cm   National Gallery of Ireland

PLATE 5

Cherry Ripe 1889

18

_Pl 5_ In this richly hued street-scene Osborne has abandoned the even, grey light of his early work. He makes dramatic use of rays of evening sunlight falling on the tops of the distant houses. It was painted at Rye, and is another example of the care with which Osborne built up his compositions with preparatory studies—in this case he even used a photograph to get an accurate record of the street.

Oil on canvas; 68.5 x 50.5 cm
Ulster Museum, Belfast

19

_Pl 6_ In Walter Osborne's early work we do not find the attachment to a particular place, typical of so many realist painters, but in the nineties, when he settled in Dublin, he was drawn to the markets area around St Patrick's Cathedral, which he haunted with his sketch pad. In pictures such as this one we feel, for the first time, the painter's sense of identification with his subjects, as he evokes the gaiety, as well as the hardship, of street life.

Oil on canvas; 59.7 x 80 cm
Hugh Lane Municipal Gallery of Modern Art

PLATE 6

Life in the Streets, Musicians 1893

20

Pl 7 **P**ainted at Foxrock, County Dublin, this is a sma[ll] plein-air *sketch, done quickly in front of the motif. Th[e] composition, while appearing direct and spontaneou[s], is put together with great skill. Nearly all of the deta[il] is concentrated in a narrow band on the horizon, a shar[p] little frieze of trees and cattle. There is a high, windy Iris[h] sky, and the foreground is cleverly articulated wit[h] clumps of grass and fluttering birds.*

Oil on board; 41.9 x 26.7 cm
Hugh Lane Municipal Gallery of Modern Art

PLATE 7

Landscape with Crows 1893

PLATE 8

Self Portrait 1894

22

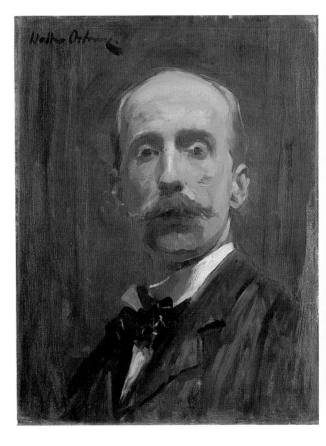

Pl 8   Aaccording *to Osborne's friend Stephen Gwynn, the pose is a characteristic one, 'intent with half-closed eyes on the canvas, the right shoulder thrown far back, the left ... forward almost like a fencer's'. He is formally dressed, as he always was in Dublin or London.*

Oil on canvas; 46 x 36 cm
National Gallery of Ireland

PLATE 9

The Goldfish Bowl *c* 1900

Pl 9   The little girl with short hair is the painter's niece
Violet. The intimacy and informality of the subject owe
something to the French impressionists, as do the coloured
shadows and the evocation of light through the use of the
full range of prismatic colour. Violet's dress is painted
with particular virtuosity, and an astonishing range of
hues evokes its vivid whiteness.

23

Oil on canvas; 76.2 x 62.2 cm
Crawford Municipal Art Gallery, Cork

PLATE 10

Mrs Noel Guinness and her Daughter Margaret 1898

24

Pl 10   **M**uch reproduced and acclaimed in its time, this is
the most accomplished of Osborne's mother-and-child
portraits. The careful finish of the faces is set off against
the virtuoso treatment of Mrs Guinness's silk dress. She
was a friend as well as a patron of the artist, which may
be why the picture is a lot less pompous than many of
his formal commissions.

Oil on canvas; 137.2 x 152.4 cm
Guinness collection

cont. from p12

communities far removed from the over-civilised cities, and, of course, by cheap living.

One of the most influential French painters of the time was Jules Bastien-Lepage, who regarded himself as a realist, and had set out to paint the realities of country life in his native Lorraine. He was fanatical about working out of doors, in front of the motif, and believed in painting in a grey, even light, so that there was as little variation as possible in the course of the day. His method of applying paint with a large brush in squarish dabs became known as the 'square brush technique', and was much imitated. In the years of his greatest success, before his death in 1884, Bastien-Lepage was followed about by hordes of young painters anxious to see him at work. Blandford Fletcher had met him in Brittany in 1882, which may explain how his work became known to Osborne, who was very much influenced by it. At Quimperlé, Osborne painted *Apple Gathering*, a picture that is in keeping with the *plein-air* work of Bastien and his followers, with its low-key palette of silvery green and grey (*Pl 2*). It was probably in Brittany in 1883 that Osborne made contact with English *plein-air* naturalists like George Clausen and Stanhope Forbes, and with Edward Stott, who was to be his frequent companion on painting expeditions for the next few years.

25

☙

ON THE MOVE

By 1884 Osborne's student days were over. For the next eight or nine years he worked mainly in England, settling in small villages which were picturesque enough to offer settings for his paintings, either inland or by the sea. His routine was to work out of doors until the cold of winter drove him back home to Dublin. It was the heyday of artists' colonies, when groups of artists would get together in some rural hamlet, living simply and painting out of doors, as French artists were doing at Barbizon, or Pont Aven in Brittany. Many of Osborne's friends and fellow students from Antwerp joined the well-known group at Newlyn, in Cornwall, which was the English equivalent of Pont Aven. Osborne may have gone there briefly, as his friend Fletcher did, but on the whole he preferred tidal rivers and mud-flats to more spectacular coastal scenery.

Shortly after their stay in Brittany, Osborne and Hill worked at Walberswick, on the Suffolk coast, a place best known through the work of Philip Wilson Steer, with whom the two became friendly. It is possible that they were drawn there by the presence of their old teacher from the schools of the Royal Hibernian Academy, Augustus Burke. It was at Walberswick that Osborne painted *An October Morning* (Pl 3).

Osborne sometimes worked inland, as he was fond of the midlands—Oxfordshire, Hampshire, Berkshire. He did not go for dramatic scenery, but for farmland, with fields, hedges and trees, and rustic-looking buildings; and he often painted the rolling downland of the south of England. Like other young and struggling artists he lived as cheaply as possible, lodging in cottages or in small country inns. He spent the summer and autumn of 1884 at North Littleton, near Evesham in Worcestershire, with Nathaniel Hill and Edward Stott—in October, in spite of the bitter cold, all three worked out of doors. In 1888 he was at Uffington, near Oxford, a pretty village of timber-framed thatched cottages nestling beneath a grassy hillside. His companion on that occasion was his friend from Antwerp, Blandford Fletcher. It was here that Osborne painted _A Cottage Garden_ (_Pl 4_).

At other times he worked on the south coast: his brother Charles was an assistant at the Winchester College Mission, St Agatha's, Landport, from 1886 to 1893, and this may have influenced his decision to travel south. He painted _Cherry Ripe_ at Rye around 1889 (_Pl 5_). He was attracted to the red tiled roofs of the area, though he felt that he had overdone the redness in this picture when he saw it exhibited in London.

BACK IN DUBLIN

Throughout the eighties, when he was spending long periods abroad, home for Walter Osborne was his parents' house in Rathmines, which he visited regularly. He was now playing an increasingly important role in the artistic and social life of Dublin. He had been exhibiting at the Royal Hibernian Academy since he was seventeen, and he continued to send his important pictures there every year until he died. He was made an Associate in 1883, and a full Academician in 1886. His rapid rise did not escape the notice of his English colleagues, and in a letter to Blandford Fletcher, the Newlyn painter Fred Hall referred to Osborne as 'the PRHA' (President of the RHA). From the early 1890s he was a popular and influential teacher at the Academy schools.

Though very much part of the artistic establishment, Osborne was one of the channels through which new European currents in art were introduced to Ireland. In 1886 he helped found the Dublin Art Club, where many of his fellow students from Antwerp, and friends and painting companions from England, exhibited.

When family responsibilities prevented Osborne from continuing to work in his English rural haunts, he turned his attention to Irish subjects, working in north County Dublin in villages like Rush or Lusk, south of Dublin at Foxrock, or further afield in Galway or Limerick. But the pictures that are most characteristic of this period were painted in the market area of Dublin, around St Patrick's Cathedral, not far from the studio he rented at 7 St Stephen's Green. They are like his earlier works, translated into an urban setting, atmospheric evocations of the shabby streets and their sad inhabitants. *Life in the Streets, Musicians* is a good example, with its group of children gathered around the musicians in the background and the marvellous still-life of brightly hued fish in the foreground (*Pl 6*).

Many of Osborne's friends were artists, and some lived in the countryside near Dublin; Osborne often went painting with them as he had with Stott and Fletcher in the eighties. He visited Nathaniel Hone at Malahide, where both men painted cows, and J B S MacIlwaine at Foxrock, where he painted *Landscape with Crows* (*Pl 7*).

Another of his friends was the writer Stephen Gwynn, who wrote the most vivid account we have of Walter Osborne as a man. Osborne emerges from Gwynn's narrative as an intensely private person who lived a life of quiet tragedy. He would have preferred to continue working in England, with like-minded artists, but growing family responsibilities forced him to spend more and more time in Dublin. The landed gentry who had commissioned pictures of their dogs and horses from William Osborne were hit by the land wars of the eighties and could no longer afford such works, so Walter's parents became more dependent on him. His brother Charles was a clergyman in the colliery districts of Northumberland, and in 1892 his sister Violet married and emigrated to Canada. Less than a year later Violet died in childbirth, and her daughter, also called Violet, was brought home to her grandparents in Rathmines. According to Stephen Gwynn, this heavy burden of responsibility meant that Walter Osborne had to turn away from the landscape and genre scenes he loved, and become a portrait painter, which was his best hope of making money. Osborne was not the sort of man to parade his private problems in public, though according to his friend Stephen Gwynn, the strain shows in the *Self Portrait* he painted in 1894 (*Pl 8*). And it was presumably because of these circumstances that he was still a bachelor at the time of his death. Yet he loved children: nearly all of his early genre scenes have children in them, and he painted his niece Violet from babyhood on, showing her with her grandparents, playing with her dolls, at tea in a neighbour's garden. In *The Goldfish Bowl* she is the little girl with short hair (*Pl 9*).

Osborne was well liked by those who knew him. He enjoyed company and liked to dine out, to drink and smoke. He moved in artistic and literary circles. Dublin at the time had a rich cultural life, with W B Yeats at its centre. Osborne was a friend of George Moore, whom he visited at his house in Ely Place. He often dined at the home of Sir Thornley Stoker, Bram Stoker's brother, also in Ely

Place. They were patrons as well as friends, and Osborne painted several family portraits for them. He was also athletic, and enjoyed cycling. Cricket was a favourite recreation. He had played for his school and was 'the most destructive kind of left-hand bowler'.

Though he no longer painted in England, he kept up with events there, visiting the London exhibitions, corres-ponding with friends, and sending his pictures to the Royal Academy and to the New English Art Club. The latter had been established in 1886 as an alternative to the Royal Academy—*plein-air* naturalists like himself were still regarded with suspicion by the traditionalists. Francis Bate, who had been a contemporary at Antwerp, was secretary for many years. The first picture Osborne showed there was *October by the Sea*, which was very much in tune with the paintings of other new English exhibitors, like Stott, Clausen and Stanhope Forbes. Later, when the character of the New English changed in favour of more impressionist work, Osborne sent pictures that fitted in with the new mood—freely handled, with vivid, adventurous colour. He kept in touch with old friends like Fletcher and Hall, and he made new ones among the leading artists of Edwardian England, among them the architect Reginald Blomfield, the sculptor Alfred Drury and the painter Alfred Parsons. In 1899 he played in a cricket match in a side that included the fashionable American painter Edwin Abbey, against J M Barrie's famous team of writers, including, on this occasion, Conan Doyle.

One of Walter Osborne's closest friends in Dublin was the art historian and critic Walter Armstrong, who became director of the National Gallery of Ireland in 1892. The two made several foreign trips together, notably to Spain in 1895. They travelled via Paris, a city which Osborne adored and which, surprisingly, he does not seem to have visited before. Even in December it was beautiful in colour and tone; he longed for his colours, and the time to make sketches. He visited the galleries, went to the circus, strolled in the Bois, and would have visited Maud Gonne, whom he had sketched in Dublin the previous month, if he had had her address. Armstrong was a considerable influence on Osborne, and seems to have been instrumental in widening his artistic horizons and in drawing his attention to the old masters, particularly the Spaniards Velázquez and Goya. This was of great help when Osborne turned increasingly to portraiture.

For the last ten years of his life Walter Osborne was best known as a portrait painter. He had to make money, and people were reluctant to buy pictures of sheep, and refused altogether to buy ones of pigs. He had always been in the habit of painting his family and friends, but now he began to accept commissions for formal portraits. Some of these are boring and stuffy, and were much criticised at the time; others were charming evocations of Edwardian women, often accompanied by their daughters, elegantly posed on drawingroom sofas, such as the portrait of *Mrs Noel Guinness and her Daughter Margaret* (*Pl 10*). He was at his best in his portraits of children, in pictures of his family, especially his mother and his niece Violet, and friends like Stephen Gwynn or J B S MacIlwaine.

Throughout the nineties Walter Osborne was gaining an increasing reputation. In Dublin he was a leading Royal Hibernian Academician. In London his pictures were hung in favoured positions at the Royal Academy, and in 1892 *Life in the Streets, Hard Times* was bought under the terms of the Chantrey Bequest as an official purchase. In 1900 his portrait of *Mrs Noel Guinness and her Daughter* was awarded a bronze medal in Paris. The same year he refused a knighthood which was offered 'in recognition of his services to art and his distinction as a painter'; it is not clear why he turned it down. He had achieved considerable powers as a painter and his style was continuing to enrich and develop itself. It was a tragic loss to art when, at the age of forty-three, on 23 April 1903, he died of pneumonia.